The French Revolution

Library of Congress Cataloging-in-Publication Data

The French Revolution
      p. cm.—(Wars that changed the world; v.3)
   Includes index.
   Summary: Examines the events of the French Revolution and how they
influenced the course of history.
   ISBN 0-86307-929-6 (set) ISBN 0-86307-934-2 (v. 3)
    1. France—History—Revolution, 1789-1799—Juvenile literature.
[1. France—History-Revolution, 1789-1799.] I. Marshall Cavendish
Corporation. II. Series.
D148.F74 1988
944.04—dc19

Reference Edition Published 1988

Published by Marshall Cavendish Corporation
147 West Merrick Road
Freeport, Long Island
N.Y.11520

Printed in Italy by New Interlitho, Milan.

Designed and produced by
AS Publishing

WARS THAT CHANGED THE WORLD

The
French Revolution

By Ken Hills
Illustrated by Angus McBride and Tony Morris

MARSHALL CAVENDISH
NEW YORK, LONDON, TORONTO

The Land of France

In 1789, France seemed the foremost power in Europe. In reality, France was a land of bad government and injustice. Wars had made France poor and taxes had to be increased to pay for them. Under French law, tax was paid by those who could least afford it, the poorer people of France. The rich paid nothing.

The poor spent all they had on food to keep alive. When taxes rose, they starved. Reforms to raise more money and raise it fairly had to be made. But the reforms were not made, so in despair the poor rebelled.

In 1789, most of the 26 million people of France worked on the land. Paris was easily the largest city. About half a million people lived there.

Rich and Poor

The French nobles who owned vast estates rarely saw them. They cared little for their lands or for the people who worked on them. Land and people were used as the source of money to pay the cost of attending the king's court at Versailles. When these costs rose, the nobles merely raised the rents they collected from their tenants.

Life was always hard for the peasants who lived on their lands. When harvests were bad it was utter misery. It was not surprising that the poor acted so cruelly towards the rich when they took command during the Revolution.

English travelers in France were shocked by the hunger and poverty of the peasants. One wrote that they looked more like hungry scarecrows than people.

Paris in 1789

The city of Paris had been the capital of France for over 800 years. In 1789, more than half a million people lived there. It was easily the largest and most important city in the country. All the major decisions which affected the lives of the people were made in Paris. The important events of the Revolution took place there. The French Revolution was, more accurately, the Revolution of Paris.

Desperate for Bread

Bread was the main food of the people of Paris. Most workers spent half their wages on it. If bread ran short the price rose, and if the price rose people starved. In 1789 the price nearly doubled. Bakeries were looted by mobs of hungry citizens. They blamed the government; soon Paris was in turmoil and ripe for revolution.

The King and his Court

The king of France was the highest authority in the land. He could rule as he pleased, either in person or through officials appointed by him. He was the source of all honors, favors and appointments craved by those next in rank to him, the high French nobility. It was necessary to be near the king and to be seen by him to receive his favors, so the nobles of France, with their hundreds of relatives, servants and hangers-on, clustered around the king to form the royal court.

The king and his courtiers lived in extreme luxury. They wore gorgeous clothes and spent their time in a ceaseless round of ceremonies and entertainments. The difference between the extravagance of the court and the misery of the common people was extreme.

PARIS

The first site of Paris was the island in the River Seine now called the Île de la Cité. Paris had grown well beyond its original boundaries and the suburbs or *faubourgs* over the walls had become part of the city by the time of the Revolution.

The king lived outside his capital at Versailles, a small country town a few miles west of Paris, in the most magnificent palace in Europe.

Louis XVI stands before the palace of Versailles, built by Louis XIV. Louis XVI became king in 1774, aged 19. Louis never liked being king. Instead of discussing affairs of state with his ministers, he spent his time hunting or carving wood. In 1770 he had married Marie Antoinette, a pretty 15-year-old Austrian princess. She did not hide her reckless and extravagant way of life. She became the most hated woman in France.

Ripe for Revolution

The ordinary people who lived in cities and towns were as badly-off as the peasants who worked on the land. They were the workers in shops and factories, the street sellers, servants, and craftsmen of all kinds.

They depended entirely on their wages for living and buying food. If prices rose they went hungry, and if they lost their jobs, they starved.

Even worse off than these town workers were the hosts of unemployed people from the countryside who flocked to the bigger towns in search of work, food and shelter. Many of them survived by begging, or by robbery and violence. These were the people who formed the mobs in Paris which began the Revolution.

IN THE COUNTRY

"The village had its one poor street, with its poor brewery, poor tannery, poor tavern, poor stable-yard for relays of post-horses, poor fountain, all the usual poor appointments. It had its poor people too. All its people were poor, and many of them were sitting at their doors, shredding spare onions and the like for supper, while many were at the fountain, washing leaves, and grasses, and any such small yieldings of the earth that could be eaten. Expressive signs of what made them poor, were not wanting; the tax for the state, the tax for the church, the tax for the lord, tax local and tax general, were to be paid here and to be paid there, according to solemn inscription in the little village, until the wonder was, that there was any village left unswallowed."

Charles Dickens
A Tale of Two Cities

Charles Dickens painted a vivid picture of the Revolution in his novel *A Tale of Two Cities.* This is an excerpt from it.

Not all taxes were collected as money. Some were paid in labor. The *corvée* was a tax which forced all peasants who lived within ten miles of main roads to work on them, and keep them in good repair. They also had to repair carriage wheels.

The Three Estates

The French people were divided by law into three groups, called Estates. The First Estate was the clergy. The Second Estate was the nobility. There were about half a million people in these first two Estates. The rest of the country, over 25 million people, made up the Third Estate. The system dated from medieval times.

When commanded by the king, each Estate elected members from all over the country to represent it. The representatives met near the king's palace at Versailles at an assembly called the States, or Estates, General. So rare was it for kings to consult their people, that a meeting had not been called for 175 years.

The States General

Now the king was desperate. After a century of extravagance the government could not find the money to run the country or pay its debts. They had attempted to raise more money by increasing taxes but they could not raise enough. The clergy and nobility refused to be taxed. Several harvests failed and there was a shortage of bread. Food riots broke out all over the country. France was ungovernable. King Louis called the States General together to air their grievances and help him solve the country's problems. They met on May 5th, 1789, but by then it was too late. The poor had run out of patience.

From the first it was clear that Louis and his ministers would not listen to the complaints of the Third Estate. Its representatives were treated like servants. They all had to dress in black and doff their hats to the nobles and clergy. They were not even allowed to use the main entrance to the assembly building, but had to come in by a side door.

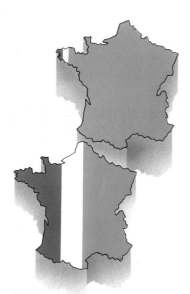

First Estate
Second Estate
Third Estate

Members of the First and Second Estates made up only about 500,000 of France's 26 million population (top), but between them sent almost as many members to the States General as the Third Estate. They also owned about 75 per cent of the land.

THE FIRST ESTATE

The bishops and priests of the Catholic Church formed the First Estate. The Church was immensely wealthy. It owned a tenth of the land and decided how much tax to pay. The clergy had many privileges. They could not be called up for military service; they had their own courts of law and they paid few taxes. Nearly all the bishops were noblemen by birth and lived lives of great luxury. The parish priests were poor and many toiled in the fields, like the members of their congregations.

THE SECOND ESTATE

The nobles of France made up the Second Estate. They varied from royal princes to poor men who worked on their own land. Rich or poor, they had special privileges, from the right to wear a sword, to exemption from certain taxes. In 1789 less than two per cent of the population were noble, yet they owned over a quarter of the land. Some titles were inherited. The king awarded the rest, sometimes in return for money, but most often through appointment to a job that carried a title with it.

THE THIRD ESTATE

The Third Estate consisted of everyone who was neither clergy nor nobility. Over 95 per cent of the French people were members of it. At the top was a small middle class of well-off tradesmen, and professionals such as lawyers and doctors. The rest, most of the people of France, varied from poor to very poor and lived as peasants in the country or as workers in the town. Whatever their position, members of the Third Estate had no privileges and no freedom from paying taxes.

11

The Revolt Begins

The voting system of the States General meant that unless one of the other Estates sided with the Third Estate they could achieve nothing. Most of the clergy and nobility supported the king, so they combined to outvote the Third Estate. The Third Estate therefore resolved to meet separately from the others.

The king prevented them from using their usual meeting place, so they gathered in a nearby Royal Tennis Court on June 20th. They declared themselves the National Assembly and swore an oath to stay together until they had changed the way France was governed. The king ordered them to leave, but they refused. Weakly, he gave in and agreed to create a new assembly. In it, the Third Estate would have a clear majority.

It was a great victory for the people, but celebrations in Paris ceased when news came that royal troops were on the move against them. The Parisians got ready to fight. Early on July 14th, a vast crowd made off with 30,000 muskets from the royal armory, and then stormed on to the Bastille prison to seize ammunition stored there.

Storming the Bastille

The Bastille was a royal fortress. There, for centuries, the French kings had locked up men without trial. It was no longer used in this way, but to the ordinary people the Bastille represented royal oppression and injustice.

The mob surrounded the Bastille and shouted to the defenders to let them in. A gun went off, and a full scale battle followed. After three hours the governor had had enough and unlocked the gates. The excited crowd rushed in and took the ammunition. The Bastille was theirs.

The storming of the Bastille (far right) on July 14th is celebrated each year as a national holiday in France.

12

The King Comes to Paris

News of the capture of the Bastille spread to the countryside where the down-trodden peasants rose against their lords. The National Assembly, in an effort to restore order, drafted new laws to do away with the old feudal order. France would, in effect, become a constitutional monarchy where the king's power would be limited by an elected government. The king would have none of these proposals, and once again the people of Paris took the law into their own hands.

A ferocious mob, made up largely of women, marched to Versailles on October 4th and invaded the royal palace. The king and his queen, Marie Antoinette, had to seek protection from the National Guard, a peace-keeping force organized by the Assembly.

Day after day the women of Paris lined up for bread, but often got nothing. Hunger made them desperate. Armed with stolen muskets, swords and spears an army of 6,000 women marched through pouring rain to Versailles to demand bread and bring the king back to Paris.

The Triumph of the Women

The next afternoon the royal family, the court and deputies of the National Assembly set out for Paris. The immense procession of 2,000 coaches, jolting over rough roads, took six hours to make the journey. It was headed by National Guardsmen, escorting wagons laden with bread and flour. Next came the king and queen with their two young children in the royal carriage. Following them trailed long lines of coaches bearing members of the court and the National Assembly. More wagonloads of bread and flour brought up the rear.

The women of Paris were everywhere, waving branches decorated with red, white and blue ribbons. Now and then they broke into song. They were happy. They had bread and they were bringing the king to Paris. It seemed the Revolution was over.

THE BRAVE QUEEN

Fearful for their children, the royal couple ordered their doors to be barred. But as the crowd of women at Versailles screamed for her blood, Queen Marie Antoinette came out alone on the balcony. Muskets were pointed at her, but no-one dared fire. The people were so impressed by her courage that their anger turned to reluctant admiration.

Fleeing to Safety

The royal family were kept in Paris for nearly two years. They grew more and more unhappy about the changes taking place in France and began to fear for their own safety. Friends planned their escape to nearby Austrian territory where the queen's brother Leopold was emperor. Disguised, they slipped out of a side door of the palace and set off for the frontier nearly 200 miles away. At Varennes the citizens blocked the way to safety. The royal family was brought back to Paris in disgrace.

War at Home . . .

In October 1791 a newly elected Legislative Assembly met. This divided into factions. The moderate members were opposed by the *Jacobins*, an extremist party led by Maximilien Robespierre, and by the *Cordeliers*, led by Georges Danton and Jean Paul Marat. These ruthless men gradually assumed power and set about stamping out all opposition. Their supporters sat in the highest part of the hall, and were known as the *Mountain*. A less extreme group called the *Girondists* sat lower down. Members who sat in the lowest, central part of the hall were known as the *Plain*.

. . . and War Abroad

Wealthy people whose houses and castles were attacked by mobs had to flee abroad. They were joined by thousands of priests and army officers who opposed the Revolution, and who could not safely remain in France. They fled to friendly neighboring countries and with the support of the authorities there settled down to plot against France and against the Revolution.

The French army was in a poor state, but anger at the activities of these traitors drove the Legislative Assembly in Paris to declare war on the countries which were helping them. By April 1792 France was at war with Austria and Prussia.

Despite his disguise, the fleeing king was easily recognized by the grandeur of his coach. But for this attempt to flee, the moderate revolutionaries might have secured a safe position as constitutional monarch for Louis.

France Becomes a Republic

THE SANS-CULOTTES

The strongest supporters of the Revolution were the workers of Paris. They despised the old nobility and the way they dressed. To emphasise this, they refused to wear breeches buckled at the knee, and instead wore pants rather like jeans. Their nickname *"sans-culottes"* means "without breeches."

Back in Paris after trying to escape, the king was kept in the Palace of the Tuileries. Then it became known that the commander of the enemy army invading France had declared he would destroy Paris if the royal family were harmed. To many French people, this was proof that the king was working with France's enemies. Far from protecting Louis, the threat had the opposite effect. On August 10th, 1792, a furious crowd invaded the Tuileries. The king and the royal family had fled for safety to the Assembly, but in the battle that followed the palace was set on fire and 600 of the king's Swiss Guard were killed.

Few people except officials used the revolutionary calendar (right), though people could be prosecuted for ignoring it.

Enraged by Louis's alleged treachery, the mob attacked the Tuileries where the king and queen had been confined as prisoners, with little privilege or dignity afforded them.

THE REVOLUTIONARY CALENDAR

Old calendar	New name	Meaning (month of)
Sept 22nd-Oct 21st	Vendémiaire	Grape harvest
Oct 22nd-Nov 20th	Brumaire	Mist
Nov 21st-Dec 20th	Frimaire	Frost
Dec 21st-Jan 19th	Nivôse	Snow
Jan 20th-Feb 18th	Pluviôse	Rain
Feb 19th-March 20th	Ventôse	Winds
March 21st-April 19th	Germinal	Sowing
April 20th-May 19th	Floréal	Blossom
May 20th-June 18th	Prairial	Haymaking
June 19th-July 18th	Messidor	Harvesting
July 19th-Aug 17th	Thermidor	Heat
Aug 18th-Sept 16th	Fructidor	Fruits

After the attack on the Tuileries, the royal family were removed to damp, cold rooms in the ancient fortress of the Temple. They were now treated as prisoners and guarded day and night.

The revolutionaries disagreed among themselves about what to do with the king. The moderates wanted France still to have a king. The extremists wanted to do away with the monarchy altogether.

"Citizen" Louis

Opposition to the king increased. A new assembly called the Convention was elected. It was full of the king's bitterest enemies. One of its first acts was to abolish the monarchy. So, on September 22nd, 1792, Louis lost the title of "King". From then on, he was called "Citizen" like everyone else.

A new age had begun, or so it seemed to the revolutionaries. To emphasize that a total break with the past had taken place, they introduced a new calendar.

The Death of the King

THE GUILLOTINE

The guillotine, used to execute the king and other victims during the French Revolution, was introduced for humane reasons. In 1791, Joseph Guillotin, a Paris doctor, proposed that not only the nobility but everyone condemned to die in France should have the right to be executed quickly and painlessly by beheading. He recommended a machine already used in other countries. It has been named the guillotine for him ever since.

The king met his death with dignity. His body was buried in an unmarked grave in a nearby cemetery. The queen was buried there, too, nine months later. The owner of the cemetery planted weeping willows on their graves to mark where they lay. In 1815, Louis' brother returned to France as king. He had both bodies reburied with great honour at the church of St. Denis in Paris, to lie with all the other monarchs of France.

Year 1 of the Republic began on the day the monarchy ended. The year was divided into 12 months of 30 days. These months were named after farming activities or weather typical of the time of year. Each month was divided into three decades of ten days. The five days left over became festivals. The extra leap year day every four years was reserved for a national celebration of the Revolution.

The new calendar was never popular. Instead of a day off every seven days, the workers had only one day off in ten. Christmas and all other religious holidays also disappeared. The system gradually drifted out of use and was formally ended by Napoleon on January 1st, 1806.

The Fatal Letters

Ex-king Louis now had only a short while to live. A discovery was made which sealed his fate. An iron box was found in the Tuileries containing letters to Louis which proved he had been plotting against the Revolution. This was the evidence his enemies had been hoping for. On December 11th, "Citizen" Louis stood before the Convention. He was accused of trying to overthrow the Revolution. After a long trial he was found guilty and sentenced to death.

At five in the morning of January 21st, 1793, soldiers of the National Guard came to take Louis to the guillotine. He tried to make a speech to the vast crowd which had come to watch him die, but drums beat to drown his words. He died with courage and dignity. The queen, called Widow Capet by the revolutionaries, was later also tried for treason and was guillotined on October 16th.

20

France in Danger

In 1793, the position of France was desperate. Major rebellions against the Revolution had broken out in the Vendée, in Lyons and at Toulon. The Austrians were advancing in the north aided by the French General who had been sent to fight them. The Spaniards in the south and the Sardinians in the south-east had crossed French borders. At Toulon the inhabitants had welcomed the British Admiral Hood. He captured the town, a vast store of arms and equipment and nearly half the French fleet without firing a shot.

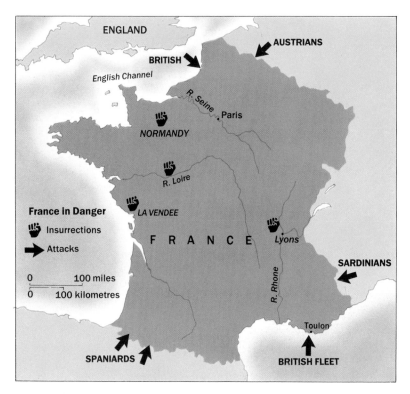

Georges Danton (above) was a giant of a man with an enormously powerful voice. He was able to dominate the disorderly, noisy meetings which took place during the Revolution. A lawyer like many other revolutionary leaders, he was only 34 when he himself was guillotined.

Revolutionary France faced counter-revolution from within and invasion by enemies. As a result its desperate leaders became ever more extreme.

The Revolutionary Committees

France had become a land of fear. The revolutionaries were afraid that traitors at home were plotting with enemies abroad to conquer France and to overthrow the Revolution. They feared too that they would all be put to death if these plots succeeded. Orders went out to set up special courts to deal with traitors. They were called Revolutionary Committees in the country. The Committee in Paris was known as the Revolutionary Tribunal.

Citizens were told to report anyone who seemed to be against the Revolution to the nearest Committee. Few of those accused in this way had a fair trial. The judges believed that the Revolution and the Republic were more important than justice. They sent thousands of people to the guillotine, nearly all of them innocent.

Nobody could hope for a fair trial from a Revolutionary Committee. Opposition was stamped out by summary execution.

The Reign of Terror

SYMBOLS OF UNITY

The Revolution gave France her blue, white and red flag. Blue and red were the colors of Paris. The royal white was placed between the blue and red before Paris turned against the king. It was a sign of unity.

"Freedom, Equality, Brotherhood" was the motto of the Revolution. Citizens were encouraged to paint these fine words on their houses. At the same time, thousands of innocent people awaited death.

The summer of 1793 to the summer of 1794 was the most terrible year of the Revolution. It was called the Reign of Terror and that is exactly what it was. There had been times of fear and violence before, but this was worse. The leaders of the Revolution deliberately used fear instead of law as a means of ruling the country.

People everywhere lived in fear of being arrested. No-one who was accused had the right to a fair trial. In Paris alone, over 2,000 people were executed during this period.

The Revolution had set out to make France a better place to live in; the Terror was now destroying it. Why did it happen? Why did the people of Paris support it?

The Committee of Public Safety

Outside Paris, the Revolution was widely hated. In particular, people were shocked by the new laws against religion. In the Vendée the peasants were at war with the government troops. France was now at war with most of Europe. The Austrians had invaded again, but many Frenchmen refused to join the army to fight them. Once again, food was short. Once more, the Paris mob rioted and raided food stores.

The government blamed these disasters on those who opposed the Revolution. They wanted all traitors tracked down and killed without mercy. A small group of determined, ruthless men was elected to carry out this task. They called themselves the Committee of Public Safety. Amongst them were Danton and Robespierre.

Crowds of people came to the executions at the guillotine. The women of Paris were always there. Many of them sat where they could get the best view, and did their knitting as they watched. Their name *"tricoteuses"* means "knitters."

Robespierre, Supreme

The revolutionaries were absolutely sure that their ideas were right. They stopped at nothing to defend them, even if it meant killing people.

Some of their ideas were very peculiar. The Revolution had abolished all religions, and for a while people were forbidden to worship God altogether. Then Robespierre, as leader of the government, invented a new religion. God was replaced by "The Supreme Being". A great Festival was held in Paris in celebration. Vast crowds attended.

Robespierre led the ceremonies. He carried a bunch of blue, white and red flowers and wore a crown of feathers. Little boys wore violets in their hair and bands played. Little girls ran about scattering flowers. Houses were decorated with red roses. Robespierre set fire to models of the evils of the world, made of straw and canvas. No-one was executed in Paris on that day. The guillotine stood idle. It was covered in velvet.

Robespierre did not look like a leader. He was small and thin. His voice was weak. His face twitched and he was near-sighted.
The terrified people of Paris rejoiced with Robespierre at his Festival of the Supreme Being (below). They rejoiced even more when his suicide attempt (right) failed to save him from the embrace of "Madame Guillotine."

The Arrest of Robespierre

The war was now going well for France and the danger of invasion faded away. Once France was safe the need for a Reign of Terror to save it disappeared. Those who had approved of the Terror sickened of it. They turned against Robespierre. He above all was responsible for it.

Robespierre's enemies sent soldiers to arrest him and his supporters. In the confusion he grabbed a pistol and tried to kill himself. He only managed to smash his jaw. In that condition he was carried on a plank before his own Committee of Public Safety. He was swiftly condemned. With his friends he was guillotined the next day.

The Reaction

AFTERWARDS

The wealthy dressed in the most extravagant fashions and went to endless parties. They behaved much like the nobles at Versailles before the Revolution. They lived for eating, drinking and pleasure. Relatives of people who had perished during the Revolution amused themselves by dressing like the victims. They went to parties with their hair tied up as though ready for the guillotine and wore thin bands of red silk round their necks.

Periods of violence and disorder are often followed by the rule of a dictator. After the Revolution, Napoleon ruled France like an absolute monarch. His imperial coronation in Notre Dame Cathedral was a magnificent spectacle.

The end of the Terror was the end of the Revolution. The nation had grown tired of it and had turned completely against its ideals and everything it had done.

Gangs of youths roamed the streets of Paris armed with whips and clubs, removing all traces of the Revolution. They dressed alike in short coats, tight trousers and boots and wore their hair long and braided at the back. It was no longer dangerous to appear to be rich.

The moderates had power in the Convention. In 1795 they planned to install a new government. But once again the people rebelled and attacked them. The official troops were outnumbered and short of experienced commanders. A 26-year-old Brigadier Napoleon Bonaparte was put in charge of the artillery to defend the building. His skilfully-placed guns drove back the advancing rebels "with a whiff of grapeshot", and caused their defeat. The new government was installed and Napoleon went on with his military career elsewhere.

The End of Confusion

Confusion and disorder continued until the army finally took over and its most successful general became ruler of France. His name was Napoleon Bonaparte and in 1804 he became not merely king, but emperor of France. He forced the pope to come to France to crown him, but at the ceremony Napoleon crowned himself as emperor, and his wife Josephine as empress, of France.

Although the Revolution itself was over, its original ideals did not die. Revolutionaries everywhere took up the motto "Freedom, Equality, Brotherhood". It has inspired all who care for freedom and justice ever since.

People and Events of the French Revolution

Barras, Vicomte de (1755-1829) Nobleman who joined revolutionaries and helped to bring an end to the Terror. Brought Napoleon to Paris.

Corday, Charlotte (1768-1793) A "moderate" revolutionary who stabbed Marat to death in his bath. Guillotined.

Danton, Georges Jacques (1759-1794) Despite his part in the Terror, this powerful leader did his best to create a just and peaceful republic. Brought to trial by Robespierre, he was guillotined.

Louis XVI (1754-1793) Grandson of Louis XV. A weak ruler who paid more regard to his wife's wishes than to the sufferings of his people. Condemned for treason and guillotined.

Marat, Jean Paul (1743-1793) Member of Paris Commune. Violent and extreme leader of the Terror whose writings fired the Paris mobs and provoked his own murder.

Marie Antoinette (1755-1793) Queen of France. A frivolous and extravagant woman, she nevertheless suffered imprisonment and death bravely. Guillotined.

Mirabeau, Comte de (1749-1791) Dissolute in his private life, this moderate but courageous leader advocated a constitutional monarchy but died before his restraining influence could be felt.

Napoleon I (1769-1821) Military genius who was called in by the Convention to clear the streets of Paris after the Terror. He did it with a "whiff of grapeshot." In 1799 he established himself as dictator of France with similar ease and put an end to the short-lived democracy.

Robespierre, Maximilien (1758-1794) Leader of the *Jacobin* faction. Notorious for his extremism, he was responsible for the deaths of thousands during the Terror. Guillotined.

1789

May — States General meets at Versailles.

June — Tennis Court Oath.

July — Fall of the Bastille.

Aug — Declaration of the Rights of Man

Oct — March of women to Versailles. Royal family and National Assembly come to Paris.

1790

June — Hereditary titles of nobility abolished.

1791

April — Mirabeau dies.

June — Flight to Varennes. Royal family brought back to Paris in disgrace.

1792

April — France declares war on Austria.

Aug — Mob attacks the Tuileries; Royal family moved to the Temple.

Sept — Prison massacres in Paris. Monarchy abolished. Year 1 of the Republic begins on September 22nd.

Nov — French defeat Austrians and advance into Belgium.

Dec — King's trial begins.

1793

Jan — King sentenced to death and executed.

Feb — War declared against England and Holland.

March — War declared against Spain. Revolutionary Tribunal set up. Revolt begins in the Vendée. Committee of Public Safety established.

April — General Dumouritz deserts to the Austrians.

July — Robespierre joins Committee of Public Safety.

Aug — Toulon taken without a fight by the English fleet.

Sept — Year 2 of the Republic begins.

Oct — Revolutionary Calendar adopted. Queen Marie Antoinette executed.

Dec — English evacuate Toulon.

1794

April — Danton and his followers executed.

June — Festival of the Supreme Being.

July — Robespierre arrested July 27th. Robespierre and his followers executed July 28th. End of Terror.

1795

April — Peace signed with Prussia and Holland.

July — Peace signed with Spain.

1796

March — Napoleon Bonaparte appointed Chief of the Army in Italy and wins victories there.

1799

Nov — Napoleon leads the government of France.

1804

Dec — Napoleon crowns himself emperor of France in Paris in the presence of the pope.

1815

Jan — Bodies of King Louis XVI and his queen re-buried in the church of St. Denis on the twenty-second anniversary of his execution.

Index

DATE DUE

11.75